DATE RETURN

THE SECOND BOOK OF SOPRANO SOLOS

compiled by Joan Frey Boytim

ISBN 0-7935-3799-1

G. SCHIRMER, *Inc.*

DISTRIBUTED BY
HAL•LEONARD® CORPORATION
7777 W. BLUEMOUND RD. P.O. BOX 13819 MILWAUKEE, WI 53213

Copyright © 1994 by G. Schirmer, Inc. (ASCAP) New York, NY
International Copyright Secured. All Rights Reserved.
Warning: Unauthorized reproduction of this publication is prohibited by Federal law and subject to criminal prosecution.

PREFACE

The eight volumes that comprise "The First Book of Solos" and "The First Book of Solos—Part II" were compiled to provide a great variety of song literature at the same basic level of difficulty for students at the beginning stages of voice study. The four volumes in "The Second Book of Solos" are designed to contribute to musical and vocal development at the next progressive level of study.

The majority of these songs require more vocal sophistication than those found in the earlier volumes. Singers using this set will be exposed to songs with wider ranges that require more vocal flexibility and vocal control, and that make greater use of the dramatic qualities of the voice. The student who can sing many of the songs in the "The First Book" and "The First Book—Part II" will be ready for the challenges found in "The Second Book of Solos."

The general format of songs remains the same as the previous collections, with a representative group of songs in English, Italian, German, and French from various periods of music history, as well as selected sacred solos. Added are several songs from Gilbert and Sullivan operettas and solos from the oratorio repertoire. Numerous pieces previously available only in single sheet form and many songs that for some time have been out of print are included.

I want to thank Richard Walters for encouraging the development of this practical song literature series. The twelve books, taken together, provide a comprehensive, inexpensive collection of 400 songs for the voice teacher and student.

Joan Frey Boytim

About the Compiler...

Since 1968, Joan Frey Boytim has owned and operated a full-time voice studio in Carlisle, Pennsylvania, where she has specialized in developing a serious and comprehensive curriculum and approach to teaching and coaching adolescent and community adult students. Her teaching experience has also included music and choral instruction at the junior high and senior high levels, and voice instruction at the college level. She is the author of the widely used bibliography, *Solo Vocal Repertoire for Young Singers* (a publication of NATS), and, as a nationally recognized expert on teaching beginning vocal study, is a frequent speaker and clinician on the topic.

M
1495
S425
1994

CONTENTS

4 ART IS CALLING FOR ME Victor Herbert
10 BESCHEIDENE LIEBE Hugo Wolf
14 LES CLOCHES Claude Debussy
17 DIE NACHT Richard Strauss
20 DOWN IN THE FOREST Landon Ronald
24 FIOCCA LA NEVE Pietro Cimara
27 HARK! THE ECHOING AIR Henry Purcell
30 HEAR MY PRAYER, O LORD Antonín Dvorák
40 LOVE'S PHILOSOPHY Roger Quilter
44 MEIN GLÄUBIGES HERZE (My Heart Ever Faithful) Johann Sebastian Bach
48 UN MOTO DI GIOJA Wolfgang Amadeus Mozart
52 MY HEART IS LIKE A SINGING BIRD C. Hubert H. Parry
62 O DIVINE REDEEMER Charles Gounod
68 OH! HAD I JUBAL'S LYRE George Frideric Handel
72 A PASTORAL Francesco Maria Veracini
57 SHEPHERD! THY DEMEANOUR VARY Brown/Wilson
78 SLEEP, GENTLE CHERUB, SLEEP DESCEND Thomas Arne
80 SONG OF THE BLACKBIRD Roger Quilter
84 A SPRING MORNING Henry Carey/arranged by H. Lane Wilson
94 THE SUN SHALL BE NO MORE THY LIGHT Dr. Maurice Greene
90 THE SUN WHOSE RAYS Arthur Sullivan
97 TAKE, O TAKE THOSE LIPS AWAY Amy Beach
100 THESE ARE THEY WHICH CAME Alfred Robert Gaul
124 TO THE BIRDS (A des Oiseaux) Georges Hüe
104 VERGEBLICHES STÄNDCHEN Johannes Brahms
34 VILLANELLE (I Saw the Swift Swallow Flying) Eva Dell'Acqua
108 DAS VERLASSENE MÄGDLEIN Hugo Wolf
110 VIEILLE CHANSON Georges Bizet
116 LA ZINGARA Gaetano Donizetti

ART IS CALLING FOR ME

(The Prima Donna Song)
from *The Enchantress* (1911)

Harry B. Smith

Victor Herbert

Copyright © 1993 by HAL LEONARD PUBLISHING CORPORATION
International Copyright Secured All Rights Reserved

hate it all, and I show it. 8va To
burn with lyr - ic am - bi - tion. Those
sing on the stage, that's the one life for me, My
ten - ors so sweet, if they made love to me, I'd
fig - ure's just like Te - traz - zi - ni; I
be a suc - cess, that I do know; And
know I'd win fame if I sang in "Bo - hème;" That
Mel - ba I'd oust If I once sang in "Faust," That

op - 'ra by Sig - nor Puc - ci - ni. I've rou -
op - 'ra so charm - ing by Gou - nod. Girls would
Poco meno
(tr)
lades and the trills that would send the cold chills down the
be on the brink of hys - ter - ics, I think, e - ven
8va
tr
8va
f Poco meno
ff
ff Pesante
(tr) (ad lib.)
backs of all hear - ers of my vo - cal frills.
strong men would have to go out for a drink.
ff
colla voce
mf dim
REFRAIN:
f
I long to be a pri - ma
I long to be a pri - ma
f
fp

don - na, don - na, don - na, I long to shine up - on the
don - na, don - na, don - na, I long to shine up - on the
stage, I have the em - bon - point to be -
stage, With my av - oir - du - pois and my
8va
sfz
come a queen of song; And my fig - ure would look pret - ty as a
tra la la la la, I would be the chief sen - sa - tion of the
page. I want to be a screech - y,
age. I long to hear them shout - ing:

* treechy
** optional lyric: "Songbirds" replacing "plump girls"

optional vocal ad lib in this section
f
That's what I'm dy-ing for, that's what I'm sigh-ing for,
8
sfz
optional Art is call - ing
port.
Art is call - ing for me.
loco
f
sffz
sffz

BESCHEIDENE LIEBE

(Modest Heart)

Hugo Wolf
English translation by John Bernhoff

Printed in the U.S.A. by G. Schirmer, Inc.

nicht dar - um; ich lie - be doch ganz ei - gen, ich lie - be doch ganz
blithe and gay, then why should I be si - lent, pray, why should I be

ei - gen.
si - lent?

mf

2. Ich bin wie an - dre Mäd - chen nicht, die, wenn sie lie - ben, hof - fen; ich
2. I'm not as o - ther las - sies are, whose love con - sists in hop - ing that

pp

rit. *a tempo*

tra - ge mei - ne Lieb' zur Schau vor al - ler Welt ganz of - fen. Oft
soon he'll come, but till he comes, sit wail-ing, weep-ing, mop - ing. How

rit. *a tempo*

hat mich schon lieb Müt - ter - lein mit dem Herz - al - ler - lieb - sten mein beim
oft has mo - ther's watch - ing eye just caught me kiss - ing him "Good bye," that's
Ko - sen an - ge - trof - fen, beim Ko - sen an - ge - trof - fen.
bet - ter far than hop - ing, or sit - ting there and mop - ing.
mf
3. Ich bin wie an - dre Mäd - chen nicht, doch glück - lich, wie ich glau - be, denn
3. I'm not as o - ther las - sies are, yet hap - py, who dare doubt it? A
pp

rit.
a tempo
mei - ne Lie - be rich - tet sich auf Trau-ring nicht und Hau - be. Er
wed - ding-ring's a wel - come thing, but I can do with - out it, un -
rit
a tempo
bleibt mein trau - ter Bräu - ti - gam, er girrt so süß, er ist so zahm_mein
til my lad, whose se - cret nest is built with - in his las - sie's breast, has
Lieb ist mei - ne Tau - be, mein Lieb ist mei - ne Tau - be.
told me more a - bout it, has told me more a - bout it.
mf

LES CLOCHES

(The Bells)

Paul Bourget
translation by Isabella G. Parker

Claude Debussy

Printed in the U.S.A. by G. Schirmer, Inc.

warn - ing, A - far through the air, Bring - ing mem - 'ry
en - ne, Ce loin - tain ap - pel Me re - mé - mo -

sweet of lil - ies a - dorn - ing Ho - ly al - tar
rait la blan - cheur chré - tien - ne Des fleurs de l'au -

rit. e dim.

fair.
tel.

poco meno mosso
(un peu plus lent)

p

dolce ed espress.
(doux et expressif)

p

These bells tell of hap - py years now o'er -
Ces clo - ches par - laient d'heu - reu - ses an -

shad - - ed And with sol - emn
né - - es, Et dans le grand
mf
tone. Once more they re - fresh the leaves that are
bois Sem - blaient re - ver - dir les feuil - les fa -
cresc.
fad - - ed, The years that are
né - - es Des jours d'au - tre -
dim.
p
gone.
fois.
a tempo
R.H.
pp
L.H.
ppp

DIE NACHT

(Night)

Herrmann von Gilm
translation by Isabella G. Parker

Richard Strauss

Printed in the U.S.A. by G. Schirmer, Inc.

beau-ty Night con-ceals, and as her du - ty Bears a-way.
Far-ben löscht sie aus und stiehlt die Gar - ben weg vom Feld.
p
Ped.
'Neath her veil doth Night en-fold
Al - les nimmt sie, was nur hold,
pp
pp
E'en the stream-let's sil'-v'ry light, And from dome and win-dow bright
nimmt das Sil - ber weg des Stroms, nimmt vom Kup-fer-dach des Doms
Ped. *
Steals the gold. Plun-der'd now the
weg das Gold. Aus - ge - plün - dert
p
dim.
pp
Ped. * Ped. *

cresc.
bush - es stand. Come thou near, I fear when
steht der Strauch, rü - cke nä - her, Seel' an
cresc.
Ped. * Ped. *
dim.
near - est, That the Night may steal thee,
See - le; o die Nacht, mir bangt, sie
dim.
Ped. * Ped. * Ped. * Ped. *
pp
dear - est, From my
steh - le dich mir
pp
Ped. * Ped. * Ped. * Ped. *
hand.
auch.
pp
dim.
sf

DOWN IN THE FOREST

Harold Simpson

Landon Ronald

Printed in the U.S.A. by G. Schirmer, Inc.

sound, Like a good ship home- - - ward bound.
f
f
dim.
Down in the for - est some- thing stirred,
dim.
Recit.
p
It was on - ly the note of a bird.
p
mf
Eb

Più lento e con molto espressione.
Now in the morn-ing of life I stand And I long for the touch of your
hand; I am here, I am here at your door, Oh
cresc.
appas-
cresc.
ff
sionato molto
love, oh, love, we will wait no
sempre f
sempre f
more!
ff e più mosso
Eb

di - mi - nu - en - do e rall.
p
Tempo I.
ppp
Down in the for - est some - thing stirred, It was
ppp
pp
on - ly the note of a bird.
p
Ped.
Ped.
Ped.
pp
Ped.
Ped.
Eb

FIOCCA LA NEVE

(Snow)

Giovanni Pascoli
English version by
Lorraine Noel Finley

Pietro Cimara

Printed in the U.S.A. by G. Schirmer, Inc.

dim.
Can-ta u-na vec - chia, il men-to sul-la ma - no.
Try-ing to soothe him, an a-ged one is sing - ing.
dim.
La vec - chia can - - - ta:
I hear her sing - - - ing:
Poco più mosso
p legato e dolce
In - tor - no al tuo let - ti - no c'è ro - se e
"A gar - den grows a - round you With ros - es
pp
gi - gli co - me un bel giar - di - no, co - me un bel giar -
bloom - ing. Lil - ies there sur-round you. Peace will soon have
poco rit.
poco rit.
col canto
Ped.
Ped.

pp
Tempo Io
di - no.
found you."
poco rit.
perdendosi
Nel bel giar - di - no il bim - bo s'ad - dor - men - ta,
Cov-ered with flow'rs, the child's young heart is drift - ing.
dim.
molto rall.
rit.
p
fioc - ca la ne - ve len - ta, len - ta, len - ta, fioc - ca la
Slow - ly the snow is fall - ing, slow - ly sift - ing, Qui - et - ly
molto rall.
col canto
rit.
pp
rit. e morendo
ne - ve, fioc - ca la ne - ve.
fall - ing, qui - et - ly drift - ing.
8
p
rit.
pp
rit. e morendo
sf pesante
pp
Ped.
Ped.

HARK! THE ECHOING AIR

Henry Purcell
Arranged by John Reed

Copyright © 1994 G. Schirmer, Inc.
International Copyright Secured. All Rights Reserved.

tri - umph sings, a tri - umph sings, a tri -

- umph, tri - umph sings, a tri - -

1
2
- - umph, tri - umph sings, sings,

And all a - round, and all a - round, pleas'd

Cu - pids clap_their wings, clap their wings, clap_their wings, pleas'd _____ Cu - pids clap their_
wings, and all _____ a - round, and all _____ a - round, pleas'd _____
_____ Cu - pids clap, __ clap, __ clap their_ wings, clap their wings, clap their wings, clap their
wings, pleas'd _____ Cu - pids clap_their_ wings. And all ____ a - wings.
1.
2.

HEAR MY PRAYER, O LORD

from the Biblical Songs

Psalms 61 and 63

Antonín Dvorák

Printed in the U.S.A. by G. Schirmer, Inc.

p
I will dwell for - ev - er in Thy tents and
pp
rit.
p
in tempo
hide me in the shad - ow of Thy wings.
in tempo
f
rit.
dim.
p
dim.
mf
Lord! Thou art in - deed my God,
mf

yea, I will seek Thee ear - ly. My soul is faint, my
bod - y long - eth, long - eth aft - er Thee
f
pp
in a bar - ren de - sert where there is no wa-ter.
pp
pp
pp

Now I will bless Thee dai - ly and lift my hands in
pray'r and ad - o - ra - tion; yea, my lips shall
f
mf
ff
poco a poco rit.
pp
praise Thee all my life long.
dim.
poco a poco rit.
pp

VILLANELLE

(I Saw the Swift Swallow Flying)

F. van der Elst
English by Alice Mattullath

Eva Dell'Acqua

Printed in the U.S.A. by G. Schirmer, Inc.

f
rit.
mf a tempo
dy - ing, where the soft breez-es are sigh - ing, where the soft breez-es are
d'ai - le, Vers le pa - ys où l'a - pel - le, Vers le pa - ys où l'a -
mf
colla voce
p a tempo
sighing, Mid bloom-ing jas-min and rose. I saw the swift swallow
pel-le Le so - leil et le jas - min. J'ai vu pas-ser l'hi - ron -
cresc.
molto dim. rit.
p
mf
fly - - - - ing, Soon she'll van - ish from my sight,
del - - - - le! J'ai long - temps sui - vi des yeux
mf
p
but in fan - cy I will fol - low, and my soul goes with the swal - low
Le vol de la vo - ya - geu - se De - puis mon â - me rê - veu - se
p

*) Breathe here eventually, when singing the high version.

f
mf
But in vain my soul was cry - ing
Et j'au - rais vou - lu comme el - le
mf
for the land the swal - low knows,
Suiv - re le mê - me che - min,
mf
I saw the swift swal - low
J'ai vu pas - ser l'hi - ron
mf
cresc.
fly - ing seek - ing sum - mer that un dy - - - - ing
del - le, Elle al - lait à ti - re d'ai - - - - le
fly - ing seek - ing sum - mer that un - dy - - - - ing,
del - le, Elle al - lait à ti - re d'ai - - - - le,

cry - - - ing
d'ai - - - le!
p
sum - mer un - dy - - - ing!
a ti - re d'ai - - - le!
mf
I saw the swift swal - low
J'ai vu pas - ser l'hi - ron -
p
fly - ing down to the South-land she goes seek ing a sum - mer un -
del - le Dans le ciel pur du ma - tin: Elle al - lait, à ti - re
cresc.
dy - ing where the soft breez-es are sigh - ing where the soft breez-es are
d'ai - le, Vers le pa - ys où l'ap - pel - le, Vers le pa - ys où l'ap-
dim.
mf
p
sighing Mid bloom-ing jas - min and rose I saw the swift swal - low
pel - le Le so - leil et le jas - min; J'ai vu pas - ser l'hi - ron -
gran cresc.

rit.
a tempo
fly - - - - ing
del - - - - le!
I saw the swift swal - low
J'ai vu pas - ser l'hi - ron -
rit.
mf
fly - - - ing!
del - - - le!
cresc.
swift - ly fly - - - ing!
l'hi - ron - del - - - le!
Ah!
Ah!
swift - ly fly -
l'hi - ron - del -
Ah
Ah!
swift - ly fly -
l'hi - ron - del -
f
tr
f
ing!
le!
animato
f

LOVE'S PHILOSOPHY

Shelley

Roger Quilter

Printed in the U.S.A. by G. Schirmer, Inc.

cresc.
sin - gle; All things, by a law di-vine, In one an-
cresc.
Ped.
Ped.
f
- o - ther's be - ing min - gle,— Why not I..... with
f
poco rit.
thine, not I..... with thine?
poco rit.
a tempo
mf
p
See, the
p
moun - - tains kiss high Heav'n,..... And the

waves clasp one an - o-ther; No sis - ter flower would be for -
- giv'n If it dis - dained its
agitato
bro - ther. And the sun - light clasps the
agitato
earth, And the moon - beams kiss the
cresc.
sea,..... What are all these kiss - - ings
cresc.
Ped.

worth,
If
Ped.
f appassionato
thou,
if
f
cresc.
ff
rall.
thou
kiss
not
ff
rall.
a tempo
me?
f a tempo
cresc.
con fuoco
ff
fff molto vigoroso
sfff
sfff

MEIN GLÄUBIGES HERZE

(My Heart Ever Faithful)

Johann Sebastian Bach

Printed in the U.S.A. by G. Schirmer, Inc.

Je - sus ist nah!
Je - sus is near!
mf
Weg Jam - mer, weg Kla - gen, weg Jam - mer, weg Kla - gen, ich
A - way with com-plain - ing, a - way with com-plain - ing, Faith
dim.
will euch nur sa - gen, mein Je - sus ist da; weg Jam-mer, weg Kla-gen, ich
ev - er main-tain - ing, My Je - sus is here; A - way with com-plain-ing, Faith
poco cresc.
dim.
p
will euch nur sa - gen, mein Je - sus ist da, mein Je - sus ist da;
ev - er main-tain - ing, My Je - sus is here, my Je - sus is here;
mf
weg
A-
cresc.

Jam - mer, weg Kla - gen, weg Jam - mer, weg Kla - gen, ich will euch nur sa - gen, mein
way with com-plain - ing, a - way with com-plain - ing, Faith ev - er main-tain - ing, My
p
Je - sus ist da! Mein gläu - bi-ges Her - ze, froh - lo - cke, sing', scher-ze,
Je - sus is here! My heart ev-er faith - ful, Sing prais - es, be joy - ful,
mf
mein gläu - bi-ges Her - ze, froh -
My heart ev-er faith - ful, Sing
dim.
p
lo - cke, sing', scher - ze, froh - lo - cke, sing', scher - ze, dein Je - sus ist da, froh -
prais - es, be joy - ful, sing prais - es, be joy - ful, Thy Je - sus is here, Sing

lo-cke, sing', scherze, froh-lo - - - cke,sing',scher - -
praises, be joy-ful, sing prais - - - es, be joy - -
dim.
- - ze, mein gläu-bi-ges Her-ze,froh-lo - cke,sing', scher-ze, froh-
- - ful, My heart ev-er faith-ful,Sing prais - es, be joy-ful, sing
p
lo - cke,sing', scher - ze, dein Je - sus ist da!
prais - es, be joy - ful, Thy Je - sus is here!
mf
cresc.
f

UN MOTO DI GIOJA

(A Moment of Joy)

English Version by Joan Boytim

Wolfgang Amadeus Mozart

Copyright © 1994 G. Schirmer, Inc.

For now will I bid a fare - well to my sor - rows, no
Spe - riam che in con - ten - to fi - ni - sca l'af - fan - no, non
rit.
long - er, no long - er such sad - ness,
sem - pre, non sem - pre è ti - ran - no,
rit.
a tempo
p
my fate turns to love, my
il fa - to ed a - mor, il
fate turns to love. A
fa - to ed a - mor. Un

mo - ment of joy that I feel in my bo - som, re - veals all the
mo - to di gio - ja mi sen - to nel pet - to che an - nun - zia di -
glad - ness of life and of love. I
let - to in mez - zo il ti - mor; Spe -
mf
p
hope that for - ev - er my sad - ness is
riam che in con - ten - to fi - ni - sca l'af -
mf
p
ban - ished, for - ev - er, for - ev - er is ban - ished, for -
fan - no, non sem - pre, non sem - pre è ti - ran - no, non
p

ev - er is ban - ished, my fate turns to love, my
sem - pre è ti - ran - no il fa - to ed a - mor, il
p
fate turns to love, for - ev - er my fate turns to
fa - to ed a - mor, il fa - to ed a -
love, for - ev - er my fate turns to
mor, il fa - to ed a -
cresc.
love.
mor.
f
p

MY HEART IS LIKE A SINGING BIRD

Christina Rossetti

C. Hubert H. Parry

Printed in the U.S.A. by G. Schirmer, Inc.

cresc.
heart is like an ap - - ple tree Whose
cresc.
boughs are bent with thick - set fruit; My
p
p
heart is like a rain - bow shell That
pad - dles in a pur - ple sea; My heart is gladder than
f
f

slower... dolce
p
all these Be - cause my love is come to
p
cresc.
me!
cresc. a tempo
f
dim.
mf
Raise me a da - is of pur - ple and gold;
mf
cresc.
Hang it with vair and pur - - ple dyes;

p
mf
Carve it in doves and pome - gran - ates, And
p
cresc. ed animando
pea - - - cocks with a hun - - dred eyes;
mf cresc. ed animando
cresc. sempre
Work it in gold and sil - - ver grapes, In
cresc. sempre
poco allargando
f
leaves and sil - - ver fleur - de - lys; Be -
poco allargando
f

- cause the birth-day of my life is come,
f
My love is come to
mf
f
mf
me.
f

SHEPHERD! THY DEMEANOUR VARY

Thomas Brown
arranged by H. Lane Wilson

Printed in the U.S.A. by G. Schirmer, Inc.

light and air - y, Dance
and sing, Dance, be
light and air - y.
f
f
f
Would you win me, you must woo As a lov - - er
ten.
mf
tr
brave and - true, Would you win me, you must woo
p
Ped.
Ped.

rall
tr
As ___ a lov - - er brave and true.
a tempo
tr
colla voce
f
rall
Slower. parlando
Hums and ha's, dull looks and sigh - ing,
p sostenuto
con Ped.
ten.
a tempo
f
tr
And such sim - ple meth - ods try - ing, Nev - er will this
rall
a tempo
mf
heart ___ sub - due, ___ I ___ must catch ___ the flame from you, Must

catch the flame from you.
p
ff
Fa la la, Fa la la la la la la
pp
Fa la la, Fa la la la la la la
ff
Fa la la, Fa la la la la la la fa la la la.
ff
sf
f
Shep-herd! thy de-mean-our va-ry, Dance and sing, be
Risoluto

light and air - y, Dance
8
and sing, Dance, be -
8
light and air - y, Dance, be
f
f
light and air - y.
Presto
colla voce
ff

O DIVINE REDEEMER

Printed in the U.S.A. by G. Schirmer, Inc.

tress! Answer me from thy throne, haste Thee, Lord, to mine
aid, Thy pit - y show in my deep anguish! Thy pit - y show in my deep
an-guish! Let not the sword of vengeance smite me, tho' righteous thine an - ger, O
Lord! Shield me in dan-ger, O re - gard me! On Thee, Lord, alone will I call.
p
cresc.
dim.
f

p
O, di-vine Re - deem - er! O, di-vine Re -
p
cresc.
deem - er! I pray Thee, grant me par - - don, and re -
cresc.
dim.
p
member not, re-mem-ber not my sins! For -
dim.
p
p
give me, O, di-vine Re - deem - er! I

cresc.
pray Thee, grant me par - don, and re-mem-ber not, remember not, O
cresc.
ad lib.
dim.
f
Lord, my sins! Night gath-ers round my soul;
colla voce.
dim.
a tempo.
f
p
f
fear-ful, I cry to Thee; Come to mine aid, O Lord!
f
p
f
p
f
cresc.
Haste Thee, Lord, haste to help me! Hear my cry,
f
cresc.

dim.
p
hear my cry! Save me, Lord, in Thy mer - - cy;
dim.
p
hear my cry, hear my cry! Come and save me. O
poco rit.
p a tempo.
Lord! O, di - vine Re - deem - - er!
poco rit.
p a tempo.
cresc.
O, di - vine Re - deem - - er! I pray Thee, grant me

dim.
par - - don and re - mem-ber not, re-mem-ber not, O Lord, my
dim.
p
sins! Save, in the day of ret - ri - bu - - tion, from
p
p
Ped.
Ped.
cresc. - -
Death shield Thou me, O my God! O, di-vine Re - deem - er, have
p
cresc. - -
Ped.
f
poco rit.
ad lib.
dim.
pp
mer - cy! Help me, my Sav - ior!
l. h.
dim.
poco rit.
f
colla voce.
pp
pp
Ped.

OH! HAD I JUBAL'S LYRE

Printed in the U.S.A. by G. Schirmer, Inc.

p
cresc.
songs like hers re - joice,
cresc.
in songs like hers re -
cresc.
poco allarg.
f
joice,
in songs like hers rejoice.
col canto
f a tempo
mf
Oh! had I Jubal's lyre, Or
p
Miriam's tune-ful voice, Oh! had I Jubal's lyre, Or Miriam's tune-ful voice, To
p
p

cresc.
sounds like his I would aspire, In songs like hers, in
songs like hers re - joice,
cresc.
f
in songs like hers re -
cresc.
poco allarg.
f
joice, in songs like hers rejoice.
a
col canto
p
p
tempo
My hum - ble strains but

p
faint - ly show How much to heav'n and thee I owe, My
hum - ble strains but faint - ly show How much to heav'n and
p
largamente
f
thee I owe, how much to heav'n and thee I owe.
Tempo I.
col canto
f
tr
tr
rall.
tr

A PASTORAL

from Rosalinda

Francesco Maria Veracini
(1690-c1750)

Printed in the U.S.A. by G. Schirmer, Inc.

wan - der, Come, dear - est, let us wan - - der; There on my pipe I'll
-net - ta; A - me - na col li - net - - - ta; Li - be - ra pa - sto -
pp
play, on my pipe I'll play, And twine thee a gar - land gay, and
-rel - la, pa - sto - rel - la, L'a - gnel - le a pa - sco - lar, L'a -
pp
mf
pp
twine thee a gar - land gay. Ah! Ah! Ah!
-gnel - le a pa - sco - lar, a pa - sco - - lar, a
tr
1.
p
2.
pa - - sco - - lar
Come,
Smor -
loco
8
8
lightly

love, for time is fleet - ing, And youth has no re -
-zar la se - te in spon - da, Po - trem del rus - cel -
- peat - ing, and youth has no re - - peat - - - - ing,
- let - to, po - trem del rus - cel - let - - - - - to;
pp
Sum - mer fades a - - way, a - -
Sen - za te - mer che l'on - da, che
- way, No long - er then de - - lay, No
l'on - da, Puó il lab - bro av - ve - le - nar, Puó il
pp

ad lib
long - er then de - - lay. Ah!
lab - bro av - ve - le - - nar. Ah!
colla voce
colla voce
rit. ad lib.
pp
O - ver the hill - tops yon - der, Come,
Me - co ver - rai su quel - la, A -
rit. colla voce
pp
dear - est, let us wan - der, Come, dear - est, let us
- me - na col - li - net - ta, A - me - na col - li -
wan - - - - der: There on my pipe I'll play, And
- net - - - - ta; Li - be - ra pas - tor - el - la, L'a -

a tempo
twine thee a gar - land gay. Ah!
-gnel - le a pa - sco - lar. Ah!
a tempo
p lightly
p
rit.
Ah! There I'll twine thee a gar - land gay, And
pa sco lar, a pa - sco - lar, L'a -
rit. colla voce
a tempo
scherzando
on my pipe I'll play, And twine thee a gar - land gay, And
-gnel - le a pa - sco - lar, L'a gnel - le a pa - sco - lar, L'a -
a tempo
lightly
p
on my pipe I'll play, And twine thee a gar - land
-gnel - le a pa - sco - lar, L'a gnel - le a pa - sco -
p and lightly

gay
-lar.
And twine thee a gar - land
L'a - gnel - le a pa - sco -
p
gay.
-lar.
ppp
slower
And on my pipe I'll play,
L'a - gnel - le a pa - sco - lar,
And
L'a -
colla voce
a tempo
twine thee a gar - land gay.
-gnel - le a pa - sco - lar.
pp
a tempo
pp
pp

SLEEP, GENTLE CHERUB, SLEEP DESCEND

from the oratorio Judith

Isaac Bickerstaff

Thomas Arne

Printed in the U.S.A. by G. Schirmer, Inc.

And o'er his sa - cred temp - les bend, bend, O bend their sa - lu - ta - ry
shade. O gent - le Che - rub, O sleep descend, descend, thy healing wings pro -
tec - tive spread, and o'er his sa - cred temp - les bend, O bend thy shade, thy sa - lu -
ta - ry shade O bend thy sa - lu - ta - ry shade.
p
pp

SONG OF THE BLACKBIRD

W.E. Henley

Roger Quilter

Printed in the U.S.A. by G. Schirmer, Inc.

espressivo.
Black-bird plays but a box-wood flute,..... But I
mp
vivo delicato.
dolce.
love him, I love him best of all .....
mf vivo
Poco più allegro e con moto.
For his song is all of the
L.H.
f
mf
joy of life, And we in the

mad spring wea - - - ther,
We two have lis - tened till he sang
molto cresc.
mp
cresc.
molto cresc.
appassionato.
allargando.
Our hearts
and
f
Ped.

poco rit.
a tempo
lips
to - ge - - - - - -
poco rit.
sf a tempo vivo e molto giocoso
Ped.
- - - - - - - - ther.
sf
f vivace
molto vivace.
mf
ff
8va

A SPRING MORNING

Henry Carey
arranged by H. Lane Wilson

Printed in the U.S.A. by G. Schirmer, Inc.

Ah!
Joy and pleas - ure
with-out meas - ure Her - alds in the love - ly spring,
Her-alds in the love - ly spring. La la la la la
la la La la la la la la la

cresc.
La la la la la la la La la la la la la la la la la la la la
cresc.
la La la la la la la la la la la la la la la.
f
ff
f
Slower
p
Gen-tle zeph - yrs, si-lent glades, Purl - ing
p meno mosso
Ped.
Ped.
Ped.

streams and cool - ing shades, Sen-ses charm - ing,
pains dis - arm - ing, Love each ten - der heart in-vades.
pp
pp
pp
f
Danc-ing, sing - ing,
mf
pi-ping, spring - ing, With our mirth the val-leys ring.

f
Ah!
Ah!
f
Joy and
f
p
pleas - ure with- out meas - ure Her - alds in the
p
love - ly spring, Her-alds in the love - ly spring.
colla voce
a tempo
mf

f
pp
La la la la la la la la La la la la
mf
pp
la la la La la la la la la la La la la la
accel.
tr
ff
la la la la la la la la La
accel.
pp
ah.
f a tempo
pp

THE SUN WHOSE RAYS

from The Mikado

words by W. S. Gilbert

music by Arthur Sullivan

Printed in the U.S.A. by G. Schirmer, Inc.

But, fierce and bold, in fie - ry gold, He glo - ries all ef - ful - gent!
I mean to rule the earth, As he the sky – We
cresc.
real - ly know our worth, The sun and I! I mean to rule the earth, As he the sky – We
dim.
rall.
a tempo
real - ly know our worth, The sun and I!
rall.
a tempo
mf
p sostenuto

Ob-serve his flame, That pla-cid dame, The moon's ce - les - tial high - ness;
There's not a trace Up - on her face Of dif - fi - dence or shy - ness:
She bor - rows light, That thro' the night, Man-kind may all ac - claim her.
And truth to tell, She lights up well, So I for one, don't blame her.

Ah, pray make no mis - take.
p
We are not shy; We're ve - ry wide a - wake!
cresc.
The moon and I!
Ah, pray make no mis-take, We are not shy; We're
dim.
rall.
ve - ry wide a - wake! The moon and I.
rall.
a tempo
mf

THE SUN SHALL BE NO MORE THY LIGHT

Dr. Maurice Greene

Printed in the U.S.A. by G. Schirmer, Inc.

mf
The sun shall be no more thy light by
p
p
mf
day; neither for brightness shall the moon give light un-to thee, neither for
mp
p
p
mf
brightness shall the moon give light un - to thee, give light un-to thee, give light un-to
rall.
mp
rall.
Andante.
f
thee: but the Lord shall be un - to thee, an e - ver-last - ing light, an
f
p
mf
e - ver-last - ing light; And thy God thy glo - - - - - ry, thy
f
p
f
mf

God thy glo - - - - ry.
The Lord shall
be un - to thee, an e - ver-last - ing light, an e - ver-last-ing light,
And thy God thy glo - - - ry, thy glo - - - -
- - - - ry, thy God, shall be thy glo - - - ry, thy God
rall.
thy glo - ry.
rall.

TAKE, O TAKE THOSE LIPS AWAY

William Shakespeare

Amy Beach

Copyright © 1994 G. Schirmer, Inc.

p
agitato
And those eyes, the break of
cresc.
più cresc.
day, Lights that do mis - lead the
morn: But my kiss - es bring a - gain,
f
f
marcato molto
dim.
Seals of love, but seal'd in vain, But my
p
cresc. molto

ff
kiss - es bring a - gain, Seals of love, but
p
f
dim.
poco rall.
a tempo
seal'd in vain.
pp colla voce
dolce marcato
dolce marcato
con due pedali
pp
Ah,
sempre pp
rit.
Seal'd in vain.
colla voce
morendo

THESE ARE THEY WHICH CAME

from The Holy City

Alfred Robert Gaul

Printed in the U.S.A. by G. Schirmer, Inc.

mf
Lamb, and have wash'd their robes;
mf catabile
Più mosso. (♩ = 88)
accel.
f
these, these are they; there-fore are they be-
cresc.
accel.
f
sostenuto
rit.
dim.
fore the throne of God, and serve Him day and night in His
sostenuto
dim.
p
a tempo
f
Tem - - ple. And they shall shine as the
p
a tempo
cresc.
f
f
bright-ness of the fir - mament, and as the stars, the
cresc.
f

stars for_ ev - er, for ev - er and ev - er, for
ev - er and ev - er, Shine for
dim.
cresc.
ev - er and ev-er, for_ ev - er and ev - er, they shall
dim.
sostenuto
a tempo
shine for_ ev - er, shine for_
rit.
a tempo
p rit.
Tempo I.
ev - er. These are they, which
a tempo
sostenuto
dim.
rit.
p

came out of great trib - u - la - tion, these are they, which
cresc.
rit.
a tempo
came out of great trib-u - la-tion,
cresc.
rit.
a tempo
and have wash'd, have wash'd their robes, and made them
cresc.
cresc.
white in the blood of the Lamb. These are
p
p
Ped.
they, these are they!
pp rit.
pp rit.
a tempo
r.h.
Ped.
Ped.

VERGEBLICHES STÄNDCHEN

(The Vain Suit)

Anton Wilhelm Florentin von Zuccalmaglio
English version by Henry Chapman

Johannes Brahms

Lebhaft und gut gelaunt
Con anima ed umore

(Er)(He)

Gu-ten A-bend, mein Schatz, gu-ten
Good eve-ning, my sweet, and good

A-bend, mein Kind, gu-ten A-bend, mein Kind!
eve-ning, my dear! Ah, good eve-ning, my dear!

p

Ich komm' aus Lieb' zu dir, ach, mach' mir auf die Thür, mach' mir auf die
I come for love of thee, So lift the latch for me, Pri-thee, lift the

pp

Thür, mach' mir auf, mach' mir auf, mach' mir auf die Thür!
latch; Lift the latch, lift the latch, lift the latch for me!

Printed in the U.S.A. by G. Schirmer, Inc.

(Sie)(She)

Mein' Thür ist ver - schlos-sen, ich lass'_ dich nicht
My_ door it is' bolt - ed, I'll not_ let thee

ein, ich lass' dich nicht ein;
in, I'll not_ let thee in!

p

Mut - ter, die räth' mir_ klug, wärst du her - ein mit_ Fug, wär's mit mir vor -
Moth - er she spoke the_ truth, Shouldst thou come in, for - sooth, All were o'er with

pp

bei, wär's mit mir, wär's mit mir, wär's mit mir_ vor - bei!
me! O'er with me, o'er with me, all were o'er_ with me!

poco f

(Er)(He)

So kalt ist die Nacht, so ei - sig der
The night is so cold, the wind is so

Wind, so ei - sig der Wind,
wild, the wind is so wild,

dass mir das Herz er - friert, mein' Lieb' er - lö - schen wird, öff - ne mir, mein Kind,
Soon will they freeze my heart, Then will my love de - part, Let me in, dear child!

Lebhafter
Più animato

öff - ne mir, öff - ne mir, öff - ne mir, mein Kind!
Let me in, let me in, let me in, dear child!

p

(Sie)(She)
Lö-schet dein' Lieb', lass sie lö - schen nur, lass sie
If it must go, let thy love be gone, let thy
f
lö - schen nur! Lö-schet sie im - mer - zu, geh' heim zu
love be gone! That it should go were best, Go home to
p legg.
Bett, zur Ruh', gu-te Nacht, mein Knab', gu-te Nacht, gu-te Nacht,
bed, to rest, So good-night, my lad! So good-night, so good-night,
gu-te Nacht, mein Knab'!
so good-night, my lad!
f
sf

DAS VERLASSENE MÄGDLEIN
(The Forsaken Maiden)

Eduard Friedrich Mörike
English translation by Joan Boytim

Hugo Wolf

Langsam

pp

Früh, wann die Häh - ne krähn,
Ear - ly the day a-wakes

eh' die Stern-lein schwin - den, muss ich am Her - de stehn, muss Feu - er zün - den.
and the stars are fad - ing, Now by the hearth I stand, kind - ling the warm fire.

pp

Schön ist der Flam-men Schein, es sprin-gen die Fun-ken; ich schau-e
Bright is the fla-ming light, the sparks are fly - ing; I gaze con-

pp *ppp*

so da-rein, in Leid ver - sun - ken.
tin - ual - ly, en-gulfed in sor - row.

pp

Copyright © 1994 G. Schirmer, Inc.
International Copyright Secured. All Rights Reserved.

etwas lebhafter
etwas ruhiger
Plötz - lich, da kommt es mir, treu - lo - ser Kna - be, dass ich die
Ah, then, it comes to me, ah, faith - less lov - er, that I have
f
f
p
p
Nacht von dir ge - träu - met ha - be.
dreamed of you, the dream is o - ver.
pp
ritard
wie zu Anfang
Trä - ne auf Trä - ne dann stür - zet her - nie - der; so kommt der Tag her - an
Tears af - ter tears now fall, blind - ing my tired eyes. So comes the day a - long,
pp
o ging' er wie - der!
o, please be end - ed!
ppp
Ped.

VIEILLE CHANSON

(Old Song)

Millevoye
English Version by Henry Chapman

Georges Bizet

Copyright, 1912, by G. Schirmer, Inc.

don — que j'au-rai fait — Que de bai - sers, — que de bai
prize — as rare as this is, What lots of kiss - es, what lots of

sers! — Si ma Lu - cet - te, si ma Lu - cet - te
kiss - es! For if my dar - ling al - ways will pay —

p

M'en don - ne deux pour un bou - quet, — J'en au - rai dix, — j'en au - rai
Two kiss-es just for a bou - quet, — I shall have ten, — I shall have

p *poco cresc.*

p *poco cresc.*

animato

dix, ah! — J'en au - rai dix pour la fau -
ten, ah! — I shall have ten for you, my

pp rall.

animato

sempre cresc.

col canto *pp*

a tempo
vet - - te.
star - - ling!
a tempo
p
p
La fau - vet - - te dans le val -
Now the star - - ling down in the
p
p
lon A lais - sé son a - mi fi - dè - le, Et tant
dell Had her - self left a faith - ful lov - er, And she
legg.
pp
fait, tant fait, tant fait, que de sa pri -
strove so hard, so hard, that it soon be -
p

son El - le s'é - chappe à ti - re d'ai - - - le.
fell, She did her lib - er - ty re - cov - - - er.
f tr
cresc.
f
dim.
Ah! dit le ber - ger dé - so - lé, A - dieu les bai-sers de Lu -
Ah! cried the shepherd in dis - may, Good - bye to kiss-es from my
p
pp
cet - te! Tout mon bon - heur s'est en - vo - lé Sur les
dar - ling! Now all my luck has flown a - way On your
pp
ai - les de la fau - vet - te! Myr -
wings, you wretch - ed star - ling! Once
p
sf poco

til retourne au bois voi - sin, Pleu - rant la per - te qu'il a
more a - hunt - ing Myr - til went, Yet sad for what he failed to
sf poco
dim. e rall.
5
a tempo
p
fai - - - - - te. Soit par ha - sard, soit à des -
get her. Ei - ther by chance or by in -
col canto
pp
a tempo p
sein, Dans le bois se trou - vait Lu - cet - - - te,
tent, In the wood, there was his Lu - cet - - - te;
rall.
rall.
a tempo
Et sen - si - ble à ce ga - ge de foi,
And so, when she saw how true was the lad,
a tempo

p
appassionato e
El - le sor-tit de sa re - traite En lui di - sant: Con-so - le -
She showed her-self and cried: My dar-ling, Myr-til, she cried, Be not so
p
appassionato e
cresc.
rall.
animato
toi, Con-so - le - toi, Myr-til, con-so - le - toi. Ah!
sad, be not so sad, Myr-til, be not so sad! Ah!
cresc.
rall.
cresc. e animato
pp
rall.
Tu n'as per - du que la fau - vet - - te!
There's no - thing lost ex - cept the star - - ling!
f
col canto
pp
a tempo
p
p

LA ZINGARA
(The Gypsy Maid)

Carlo Guaita
English Version by Theodore Baker

Gaetano Donizetti

Copyright, 1901, by G. Schirmer, Inc.
Copyright renewal assigned, 1929, to G. Schirmer, Inc.
Copyright, 1941, by G. Schirmer, Inc.
International Copyright Secured
Printed in the U.S.A.

man - to del cie - lo, mia ma - dre e - sul - tan - do la
sky bright - ly beam - ing, 'Twas there that my moth - er my
a tempo
vi - ta mi diè.
life gave to me.
Fan -
As
a tempo
f
p
ciul - la sui grep - pi le ca - pre e - mu - la
child, on the moun-tain I fear-less - ly rev
i, per vil - le e cit - ta - di cre - sciu - ta dan - za
elled, As maid-en, I danced in the towns while we trav

i, le da - me lor pal - me di - ste - se-ro a
elled; To la - dies their for - tune I told for a
p
legg.
cresc.
me. La ra la, la ra la, la ra la, la ra la, La ra la, la ra la,
fee. La ra la, la ra la, la ra la, la ra la, La ra la, la ra la,
p
cresc.
p
la ra la ra la, la, la, ah!
la ra la ra la, la, la, ah!
f
p
f
La zin - ga - ra, la zin - ga - ra!
The Gyp - sy - maid, the Gyp - sy - maid!
ff

p
Io lo - ro pre - dis - si le co - se non na - - -
All things I re - vealed that should come on the mor - - -
p
- - - te, ne fe - ci do - len - ti, ne fe - ci be -
- - - row, Fore - tell - ing of glad - ness, fore - tell - ing of
a - - - te. Se -
sor - - - row; And
p
gre - ti co - nob - bi di sde - gno e d'a -
se - crets of ha - tred and love, too, I

p
cresc.
mor, La ra la, la ra la, la ra la, la ra la, La ra la,
told, La ra la, la ra la, la ra la, la ra la, La ra la,
p
cresc.
la ra la, la ra la ra la, la, la,
la ra la, la ra la ra la, la, la,
f
p
ah! La zin - ga -
ah! The Gyp - sy -
p
f
ra, la zin - ga - ra! Ah Un
maid, the Gyp - sy - maid! Ah One
p

Un poco meno mosso
gior - no la ma - no mi por - se un don -
day came a youth that his fate I shall
p
zel - lo, mai vi - sto non fum - mi gar -
tell him, So gal - lant, so kind - ly, so
p
f
zo - ne, gar - zo - ne più bel - lo, oh s'ei nel - la
kind - ly, that none might ex - cel him; Ah, read he my
p
pressando
pressando
cresc.
f
de - stra leg - ges - se - mi il cor, oh
heart in the hand he did hold! Ah,
cresc.
f
fp

calando
s'ei nel - la de - stra leg - ges - se - mi il
read he my heart in the hand he did
calando
f
pp
cor! La zin - ga - ra! ah!
hold! The Gyp - sy - maid! Ah!
fp
f
p
la zin - ga - ra! ah!
the Gyp - sy - maid! Ah!
f
p
f
p
la zin - ga - ra! ah!
the Gyp - sy - maid! Ah!
fp
p

rall.
rall. poco a poco
ah!
Ah!
rall. poco a poco
Ossia
rall. più
pp
tr
tr
la zin - ga - ra! ah!
the Gyp - sy - maid! Ah!
a tempo
la zin - ga - ra!
the Gyp - sy - maid!
a tempo
f
ff

TO THE BIRDS

(A des Oiseaux)

Eugène Adenis
English version by Louise Baum

Georges Hüe

Printed in the U.S.A. by G. Schirmer, Inc.

rush - - es, Set the fields a - flush with May!
ret - - tes Et les fleurs des verts buis - sons!
mp
While in hap-py cheer you hov - - er, Pret-ty birds, so brave and
Tou-jours votre âme est en fê - - te, Gais oi-seaux qu'on aime à
bright, To the po ct and the lov - -
voir, Pour l'a - mant et le po - è - -
mf
er, Sing your song at dawn or night! O - ver
te, Vous chan - tez ma - tin et soir! Mais dans
p

yon-der in the heath-er, They have hid a cru - el snare; Swing in cir-cles there to-
la plaine, il me sem-ble Qu'on a ten-du des ré - seaux; Vol - ti - gez tou-jours en-

geth - - er, But, com - rades, Oh, have a care!
sem - - ble: En gar - de, pe - tits oi - seaux!

p *mf* *mp*

mf

Dip and dive a - bove the stub - ble, But a-
Penchez-vous sans toucher ter - re, Voy-ez-

mp

cresc. poco a poco

light not, for they wait! They will get you in - to trou-ble, Lure you to a sor - ry
vous au coin du bois, Vous guet - tant a - Cec mys - tè - re, Ces en - fants à l'œil sour-

cresc. poco a poco

f
mp
fate.
Flee, Oh, flee them! do not
nois?
Ah, bien vite à ti - re
f
mf
p subito
mf
rall.
a tempo
fol - - low! O quick, O quick, wing you wide! But come,
d'ai - - le, Fuy - ez, fuy - ez leurs ap - pâts; Ve - nez
rall.
a tempo
mf
p
trust-ful as the swal - - low, Who darts and pois - es at my side!
a - vec l'hi - ron - del - - le, Qui, dans son vol, suit mes pas.
In my gar-den, safe-ly bid - - ing, Ev - 'ry
Dans mon jar-din nul-le crain - - te; Vous pour-
mp

beak my or-chard shares, You may pil-lage free from chid - -
rez, d'un bec lé - ger, Pil - ler, pil - ler sans con - train - -

p

ing, My cher-ries ripe, or my pears. Now, good-night, you pret-ty
te, Tous les fruits mûrs du ver - ger. Bon-soir, bon-soir les fau-

rall. Più lento *pp*

rall. *pp*

thrush - es, With your songs at close of day, Lull to sleep
vet - - tes, Bon-soir les joyeux pin-sons, En-dormez

p *p*

the brook-side rush - - es, And the fields a - flush with May!
les pâ - que - ret - - tes Et les fleurs des verts buis-sons!

p *rall.*

rall. *pp*